# Jesus Heals
# a Little Boy

## A Miracle in Capernaum

### Jim Reimann

### Illustrations by Hayim Roitblat Otsarya

Jesus returned to Cana, where he had turned water into wine,

When a royal leader said, "My child is sick, he's a son of mine."

He begged Jesus to go home with him to Capernaum by the sea,

"Please come heal my dear child, and save him from death, is my only plea."

4

Christ said, "You will not believe till you see miracles with your eyes,"
To which the man begged once again, "Sir, please come before my child dies."
Jesus said, "You may go. Your son will live," and power imparted;
So the man took Christ Jesus at His word and quickly departed.

While the royal official headed home, and was well on his way,
His servants coming from Capernaum met him, with something to say.
"We have amazing news for you; Your boy is living and well,"
A message for the man that was a wonderful joy to tell.

"When did my son take a turn for the better?" the man asked his men;

"Yesterday, the seventh hour," they quickly answered, "It was then."

The father realized it was the exact time Christ Jesus had said,

"Your son will live"–that the high fever had left his son in his bed.

The man had new faith, and now he and his whole family believed,
Trusting in the Lord God and turning from sin, Jesus they received.
So this little boy was saved from more than simply being ill,
His body was well, and God entered his heart, forever to fill.

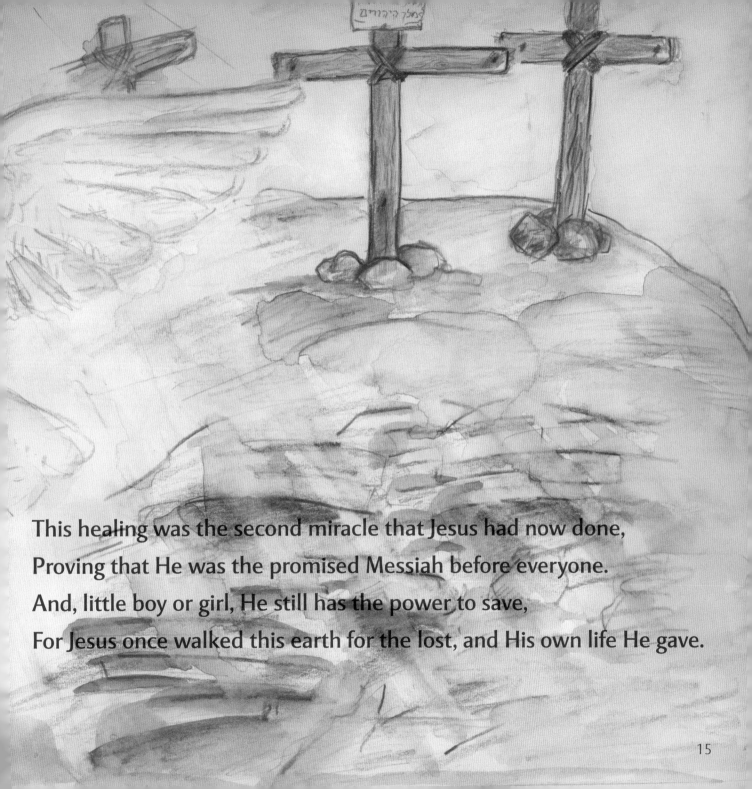

This healing was the second miracle that Jesus had now done,
Proving that He was the promised Messiah before everyone.
And, little boy or girl, He still has the power to save,
For Jesus once walked this earth for the lost, and His own life He gave.

Rev. Jim Reimann
Israel Tour Leader of 25+ Pilgrimages
Editor of the Updated Editions of:
*My Utmost for His Highest* (Oswald Chambers)
*Streams in the Desert* (Lettie Cowman)
*Morning by Morning* (Charles Spurgeon)
*Evening by Evening* (Charles Spurgeon)

ISBN: 978-965-7607-22-0

Printed by ⚡ GESTELIT
info@gestelit.co.il
Printed in the Holy Land

**For ordering information, please contact the publisher:**
Intelecty, Ltd.
76 Hagalil
Nofit, Israel 36001
Tel: 97249930922
Fax: 972722830147
Mobile: 972523348598
galit@gestelit.co.il
jesusbooks4kids.com

# Also in this series:

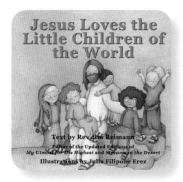

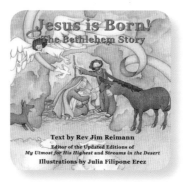

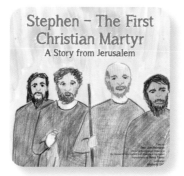

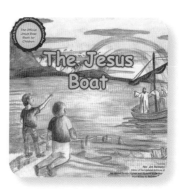

John 3:16
Jesus and Nicodemus in Jerusalem

Text by Rev. Jim Reimann
Editor of the Updated Editions of
*My Utmost for His Highest and Streams in the Desert*
Illustrations by Julia Filipone Erez

NO POTATO
NO TOMATO
Life in the Time of Jesus

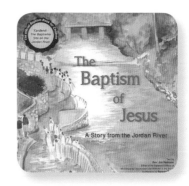

The Baptism of Jesus
A Story from the Jordan River

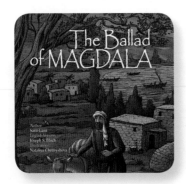

The Ballad of MAGDALA

Author:
Sarit Gani
English Version:
Joseph S. Bloch
Illustrations:
Nataliya Chernysheva

Caesarea~
A Glimpse at the Past of a Glorious City

English Version: Joseph S. Bloch
Illustrations: Nataliya Chernysheva

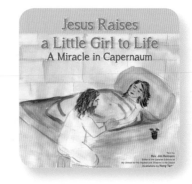

Jesus Raises a Little Girl to Life
A Miracle in Capernaum

Rev. Jim Reimann
Editor of the Updated Editions of
My Utmost for His Highest and Streams in the Desert
Illustrations by Rony Tier

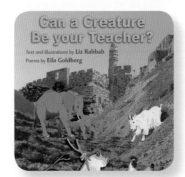

Can a Creature Be your Teacher?

Text and illustrations by Liz Rabbah
Poems by Eila Goldberg